How to Plan a WINNING Campaign

DrewMcKissick.com
Campaigns, Opinions & Activism

Helping Conservatives Make a Difference!

"How to Plan a Winning Campaign"

Copyright 2013 by Drew McKissick

Other books by Drew McKissick:

- The Beginner's Guide to Grassroots Politics
- The Intermediate Guide to Grassroots Politics
- The Advanced Guide to Grassroots Politics
- Nine Conservative Grassroots Opportunities

Visit http://drewmckissick.com/my-books/ to find out more!

Table of Contents:

INTRODUCTION

Before you get started on any campaign – whether it's an election campaign or an issue based campaign – you *NEED* to have a plan. If you do the planning you need to do on the front end, you'll save yourself a lot of time and headache later, not to mention increase your chances of being successful.

Remember, "fail to plan, plan to fail".

This is not about "running" a campaign, (that's another book), but rather about how to plan one – and how to do the research and make the evaluations that you will need to make in order to decide what kind of strategy and tactics you should use.

So, where do you start? That's what this book is about. It's written to help you go through a step-by-step process of doing the things you need to do, in the general order you need to do them, to develop a plan for your campaign.

> *"Plans are useless, but planning is indispensible"*
> *– Gen. Eisenhower*

Once you've got a plan, it makes it much easier to know "what's next" on a day to day basis, and it's easier to determine what you should do, based on what you have determined is important. It will give you confidence as you go forward because you will have thought things through, and you'll know "why" it's better to do things this way or that, not just guess or roll with the flow.

We will break this out into five basic areas:

1) **Evaluation:** determine the factors that relate to your objective (how things impact "winning")
2) **Research & Targeting:** analyze your capability of achieving the results you want (based on the research that you do)
3) **Strategy:** develop a strategy that maximizes your strengths and their weaknesses
4) **Tactics & Implementation:** determine what tactics to use and when
5) **Regular Review:** evaluate and review the plan and your progress on a regular basis

When you're ready, get started simply by following the "Planning Checklist" and use it to keep track of things until you're done. As you pull information together, whether writing notes, using a word document or spreadsheets, etc., check each item off and then make it easy on yourself by keeping everything in one place, such as in a notebook.

Don't try to plan in a hurry. If the purpose is to develop a *good* plan, then you need to respect that process and take the time necessary to do it right. Depending on how much time you have available, or who else may be helping you, you could spend several weeks on doing it right.

Don't expect what you do to be perfect. No plan ever survives contact with the enemy. The point is to go through the process, have as good of a plan as you can because of it and then review, improve and adjust as you go.

Take your time and don't take shortcuts. You'll be glad you did it right.

PLANNING CHECKLIST

Evaluation

- ☐ Candidate information
- ☐ Political environment
- ☐ Issue analysis
- ☐ Resources analysis
- ☐ Media analysis
- ☐ Surveys

Research & Targeting

- ☐ Geographic Information
- ☐ District Information
- ☐ Electoral research
- ☐ Turnout projections
- ☐ Targeting
- ☐ Vote goals
- ☐ GOTV goals

Planning & Strategy

- ☐ Initial assumptions
- ☐ Strategic review
- ☐ Theme development
- ☐ Strategic objectives
- ☐ Strategy statement
- ☐ Review

Tactics & Implementation

- ☐ Organizational structure
- ☐ Message development / Communications
- ☐ Advertising
- ☐ Phone banks
- ☐ Coalitions
- ☐ Finance and budget
- ☐ Timeline

Are there any immediate priorities that need to be addressed quickly? *Create a to-do list of any short-term priorities while comprehensive planning is underway, especially if your election timetable is short, (ex. basic message points, draft copy, announcement venue and timing, attendees, mailer, e-blast, video, endorsements, schedule issues).*

EVALUATION

To get started, the first thing you need is a clear-eyed evaluation of the things that will have an impact on the campaign. This includes the candidates (or the "issue" for an issue ballot or lobbying campaign), the current political environment, the issues, the media, and available resources.

CANDIDATE INFORMATION:

Take a good look at the opposition as well as your own campaign from several different perspectives, then specifically focus on doing more detailed research of the opposition. (You can use the "Candidate Profiles" spreadsheet in this section and note either with a "check mark" or an "x" if things are favorable or not)

Candidate Profiles:
- ☐ Biography / Resume
- ☐ Personal strengths and weaknesses
- ☐ Stands on the Issues (any flip-flops or philosophical problems?)
- ☐ Support from special interests
- ☐ Political experience
- ☐ Past campaigns
- ☐ Financial support
- ☐ News clippings

> *"If you know the enemy and know yourself you need not fear the results of a hundred battles."*
> *– Suz Tzu*

Opposition Research: It should answer two basic questions: where do they stand, or where have they stood versus what they claim? And, if they are an incumbent, what have they sponsored or co-sponsored?

- ☐ **Check the following items:**
  - Votes and/or stands on issues: are they consistent?
  - Accomplishments: have any of their proposals become law?
  - Attendance records
  - Campaign and personnel finance disclosures: (look for any position switches within days of getting major contributions)
  - Any resume inflation?

Candidate Profiles

BIOGRAPHICAL INFO:	Us	Them
Residency / how long?		
Age		
Marital status		
Children		
Education		
Occupation		
Family assets / liabilities		
Club / other memberships		
Awards / honors		
Civic involvement		

STRENGTHS & WEAKNESSES	Us	Them
Public speaking ability		
Understanding of issues		
Temper		
Personal looks		
Charismatic or dull?		
Arrogant or self-effacing?		
Good campaigner?		
"Fits the district"?		

STANDS ON ISSUES:	Us	Them
Education		
Jobs		
Roads		
Environment		
Abortion		
Crime		
Taxes		
Health care		
Others?		

SPECIAL INTERESTS:	Us	Them
Chamber of Commerce		
Home builders		
Realtors		
Unions		
_____		
_____		

EXPERIENCE:	Us	Them
Party involvement		
Past political experience		
Elected offices held		
Voting record		
Attendance record		
Public statements		
Media relations		
Accomplishments		
Promises not kept		

PAST CAMPAIGNS:	Us	Them
Full time or part time?		
Any campaign staff?		
Internet / Email?		
Direct mail?		
Radio?		
TV?		
Door to door?		
Type of campaign literature		
Polling / survey research?		
Debates?		
Good campaign org?		
Quality endorsements?		
Candidate's image?		

FINANCIAL SUPPORT:	Us	Them
Past total raised?		
Past total spent?		
Spent well?		
Total number of contributors		
Who were large donors?		
Candidate loans?		
What PAC's contributed?		
Party contributions?		
Current financial support:		
_____		
_____		
_____		
_____		

Make copies and give to others who are helping you with the review!

Another Grassroots 101 e-book from DrewMcKissick.com – Copyright 2013 - Connect on Twitter @DrewMcKissick

POLITICAL ENVIRONMENT:

Whether you like it or not, there are some outside factors that aren't related to you or the opposition that will have an impact on your campaign. **You *need* to take them into account and determine what kind of impact they will have.** Below is a short list of items to consider, but make note of anything that could have a major impact.

☐ **List any outside influences that may impact the race**
- National / state / local politics and elections?
- Incumbent president on the ballot? Are they popular?
- Incumbent governor or senator on ballot? Are they popular?
- Any key referendums on the ballot?
- Economic conditions?
- Major endorsements? (Who's supported by the big names, and will it matter?)
- Candidates for other races likely to draw a more favorable or unfavorable electorate?
- Major special interest groups or coalitions at work? Will they help or hurt?
- Who can you expect to work against you?

ISSUES ANALYSIS:

Take a look at the issue environment and identify important issues, those that are getting attention, those that aren't, etc. **Determine which issues will have the greatest impact on your campaign,** (or could if they caught fire).

"Issues win campaigns"
- Lee Atwater

You can check any recent polls that have been done that mention specific issues, make note of those that get a lot of play in "letters-to-the-editor", consider doing a "focus group" of campaign supporters and reviewing major issues with them, or even send a web-based "issues survey" or poll to everyone on your email lists.

☐ List the "hottest" issues?
☐ List issues that have the potential to be "hot"?

RESOURCES ANALYSIS:

A good campaign plan will try to get the greatest benefit out of all available resources. In order to do that, you first have to identify them – which means taking an "inventory" of all actual and potential resources that you have access to.

☐ **Create a "Resource Inventory" list** *(use list below or create your own spreadsheet)*

Assets	Asset Type	Quantity	Available?
Donor list	Phone / Direct Mail		
Activist list (non donors)	Phone / Direct Mail		
Campaign email list	Email		
Facebook	Social media		
Twitter	Social media		
Candidate personal email list	Email		
Personal Facebook	Social media		
Personal Twitter	Social media		
Possible Assets:			
Other donor lists?	Phone / Direct Mail		
Other email lists?	Email		
Other Facebook?	Social media		
Other Twitter?	Social media		
* List everything you might get access to			
* Begin regular process of asking for access and/or sharing of links			

MEDIA ANALYSIS:

Communications are a critical part of any campaign and, like it or not, that means dealing with the media, (both the "old" and "new" varieties). In order to do that effectively you need to gather some basic information about who you will be dealing with.

- ☐ **List all media outlets that would conceivably cover the campaign: ex. radio, TV, newspapers, blogs and other notable outlets.**
  - List key contact information, political ad rates, deadlines and endorsement policies

- ☐ **Determine which outlets will be most relevant to the campaign and how to use them**
  - (Ex., blogs, Facebook, Twitter, Supporter social media accounts, etc.)

- ☐ **ID and create a list of key social media contacts** (ex., media, bloggers, key "influentials").
  - o Communicate and share campaign updates with them on a regular basis

> *"It's the responsibility of the media to look at the president with a microscope, but they go to far when they use a proctoscope."* - Nixon

DISTRICT SURVEY:

If your campaign is in a financial position to have a professional survey done, you'll want to make sure that it provides information that will allow you to break things down as follows.

- ☐ What is the level of name recognition of the candidates.
- ☐ What is the public opinion of the candidates? (% favorable vs. % unfavorable?)
- ☐ What are the "horse race" numbers? (% for vs. % against?)
- ☐ What are the demographics of supporters?
- ☐ What are the demographics of undecideds?
- ☐ Which issues are "hot" / which are not?

ELECTORAL RESEARCH AND TARGETING

Over two-thousand years ago, the Chinese General Sun Tzu explained what he called the Five Elements of the Art of War as follows:

1. *Measurement of space*
2. *Estimation of quantities*
3. *Calculations*
4. *Comparison*
5. *Chances of victory*

He stated that: *"Measurement of space is derived from the ground. Quantities derive from measurement, calculations from quantities, comparisons from calculations and victory from comparisons."*

> *"The successful warrior is the average man, with laser-like focus."*
> — *Bruce Lee*

To put that in political terms, you need to evaluate the environment, research the numbers, determine what's needed to win, compare yourself and the opposition and realistically estimate if you can win.

Before you can move forward with making an actual plan, you start by collecting some basic information, specifically previous election returns and demographics, and breaking those numbers down to the precinct level to get a better idea of how they look and where you can find the votes to win.

GEOGRAPHIC INFORMATION:

Get copies of maps of the areas you'll be campaigning in, (ex. a district map with precinct boundaries overlaid on it). Pin it on the wall. This will make it easier to visualize things and make important notations as you go forward.

- ☐ District Maps
- ☐ Precinct Maps

DISTRICT INFORMATION:

Below is a list of the information that you will need to base your research in this section on:

- ☐ Get voter registration figures, (by race, precinct, sex, etc.)
- ☐ Get previous election returns, (for same "type" election: ex. "presidential" or "off year" election)
- ☐ Make a list of important special voter groups & organizations: *(i.e.. farmers, union members, sr. citizens, minorities, teachers, veterans, civic, professional and religious organizations, etc.).*
- ☐ Get Census information: households, (#'s in each); average income, race, sex, education, occupation, owners/renters, religion, home values, length of residence, total over 18.

ELECTORAL RESEARCH:

This is where using a spreadsheet saves you a lot of time. By listing the names of the precincts down the side, and key figures (like those below) across the top, after you enter the information you can then sort the page by any column in order to identify priorities. The results should show these key statistics for each precinct, as well as a district wide "total" at the bottom.

Determine the following raw numbers and percentages on a precinct basis in the district:

☐ Determine the Base Republican number (Use the Republican that received the fewest votes in each precinct – be careful not to prejudice this by using a race with special circumstances)

☐ Determine High Republican number (Republican with the highest level of support)

☐ Determine Switch vote by precinct by subtracting Base from High vote

"If we knew what it was we were doing, it would not be called research, would it?" - Albert Einstein

☐ If your state has partisan registration, add columns for Republican and Democrat figures

☐ ID heavy total registration areas, (as % of 18+ pop)

☐ ID heavy total turnout areas, (as % of reg. voters)

☐ Identify "sex" and "race" demographics of: (population, registered voters & voters)

NOTE: *"high" and "switch" vote info is only needed for general election campaigns*

MAKE PROJECTIONS:

Now you need to determine how many people are likely to show up and vote on Election Day. This is where you take past voter turnout into account and apply it against current voter registration figures and make projections.

☐ **Create voter turnout projections**
- List past "voter turnout" and past "voter registration" figures by precinct.
- Divide "voter turnout" by past "voter registration" to determine what % of the registered voters actually voted. (note: differentiate between national and state election years).
- Apply that % to current registration figures to obtain "projected turnout" per precinct. (Again, be sure you're projecting a similar "national" or "state" election)

☐ **Create "Base" and "Switch" vote projections** (for general elections)
- Determine the projected "Base" vote by multiplying "projected turnout" by the "Base" percent you identified earlier.
- Determine the projected number of "Switch" votes by multiplying "projected turnout" by the "Switch" vote percent you identified earlier.

TARGETING:

If everything is important, then nothing is important. If you focus everywhere, then you're not focused. In any campaign, you have to work with what the electorate gives you, but **targeting is a way of identifying the areas and voters who matter most to the campaign** so you will know where to focus in order to get the most out of your resources.

Party Primaries: Targeting in primaries is easier compared to general elections. Simply identify which precincts provide how many votes in the average primary. Focus in those areas. In addition to targeting individual voters in previous primaries, you can target (resources permitting) non-voters in precincts with really high GOP primary turnout and/or high "base" support for Republicans in general elections, (since the odds are that these voters are Republicans as well).

☐ **For Republican primaries, rank precincts by:**
- Their % of total GOP primary voters

General Elections: In most cases your targeting plan in a general election will need to be broader than just focusing on Republicans. That means taking into account "switch" voters and Democrats.

☐ **Perform the "50%+1" Equation":** (which precincts can you focus on that will provide the votes you need to win?)
- Is the "Base" vote over 50%? If so, rank all precincts on that basis and then focus on the precincts that delivered that vote.
- If not, is the "High" vote over 50%? If so, rank all precincts on that basis and then focus on the precincts that produce the bulk of that vote, (will include "base" plus "switch" precincts).
- If not, do the above plus concentrate on locating areas with large contingents of conservative Democrats/ or where they potentially live, via demographic profiles.

> *Targeting is a way to determine where you should (and shouldn't) spend your time and money – don't neglect it.*

☐ **Group ID: categorize and then prioritize the precincts as follows:** (This tells "how" to go after – or ignore – certain areas)
- **GOP CORE** = large <u>base</u> % / large <u>high</u> % / small <u>switch</u> %
- **SWITCH** = Small <u>base</u> % / large <u>high</u> % / large <u>switch</u> %
- **DEM CORE** = Small <u>base</u> % / small <u>high</u> % / small <u>switch</u> %

NOTE: You can also cross-reference these precincts with the demographic profile and voter registration information to get a better idea of how to approach them.

DETERMINE VOTE GOALS:

Now that you've done your research, estimated the probable voter turnout and identified the areas that are most important to you, it's time to set some goals and determine how many votes you realistically think you can get from each area.

Party Primaries: In primaries you're only targeting Republicans, and you may well have more than two candidates running…which means you may have a runoff. So you need to make a rational decision about vote goals. Is there a previous similar election you might look to for guidance? A previous campaign that resembles yours when it comes to resources and the type of supporters?

☐ **Identify enough potential votes to win**
- Evaluate projected turnout and target enough precincts to be able to get a reasonable percent of the vote in them to be able to get more than 50% of the vote district wide.

- Make note of precincts that underperform in terms of their total percent of GOP primary vote relative to their percent of total voters. If they have a high "Base" vote, the odds are that you can mine those precincts for increased primary turnout.

General Elections: Once again you have to approach general elections differently. First, find out if you can win with just Republicans. If not, your vote goals will have to be broader.

☐ **In areas with a previous <u>same level</u> GOP victor, in the <u>same type</u> of election year:**
- Select similar level race where GOP won by <u>at least 52%</u> and determine the percent of the vote achieved in each precinct, then multiply that percent by the raw number of projected turnout. The result equals the <u>Vote Goal</u> for that area.

☐ **In areas with <u>no</u> previous <u>same level</u> GOP victor:**
- Add the <u>"Base"</u> + "Switch", then multiply that percentage by the raw number of projected turnout. The result is the <u>Vote Goal</u> for that area.

If the resulting total projected vote goal is not greater than 50% of the projected turnout, then you will need to review and see which areas you think you can realistically adjust upwards in order to find enough votes to win.

☐ **Prioritize precincts within the "3 categories" by vote goals, ("GOP", "Dem", "Switch").**

NOTE: When reviewing your numbers, consider:
- *Was there a coattail effect (or headwind) due to ballot issues or other candidates? Will there be?*
- *Have there been big population changes since the election #'s you're using?*
- *Make sure vote goals provide enough votes to win, but aren't so high that they discourage workers*

GOTV GOALS:

A "Get out the vote" goal should represent and actual target number that the campaign can ensure turnout of (ex. 15% of "vote goal"), whether through rides to the polls or phone calls to verify that they actually voted.

☐ **Create a separate GOTV column on the spreadsheet and multiply the "vote goal" by 15%.**

NOTE: Color-code the precincts within the district map and/or spreadsheet by the "3 categories" (GOP, Dem, and Switch) to make your priorities stand out.

PLANNING & STRATEGY

Now that you've got your initial evaluations done and have looked at the numbers and created your projections and goals, you're ready to take all of this information together and make some assumptions and ask some questions. The result will help you begin to form a strategy.

INITIAL ASSUMPTIONS:

Review the information you've put together so far and do the following:

- ☐ Identify the strengths and weaknesses of each campaign (based on the candidate profiles/comparisons spreadsheet.
- ☐ Review electoral and demographic profiles and the potential impact of other political forces, media analysis, targeting results and "Resources" list. (Do you need more info, research or polling?)
- ☐ List all assumptions drawn from this review. (Make note of everything that hurts or helps)

> *"Everybody has a plan until they get punched in the face"* – Mike Tyson

STRATEGIC REVIEW:

Answer the following questions:

- ☐ What are the main issues in the race?
- ☐ What are the key reasons for supporting our candidate/campaign?
- ☐ What are the key reasons for denying the job to the opposition?
- ☐ How do we want our candidate/campaign to be perceived?
- ☐ How do we want the opposition to be perceived?
- ☐ What is the philosophical thrust of the campaign, or will there be one?
- ☐ What is our opposition's strategy?

THEME:

When you look at the answers to the questions above, you should see a general theme beginning to develop.

- ☐ **Determine an overall "umbrella" theme that could tie it all together**
  - It should speak to a shared concern that matches your candidate/campaign's qualifications to remedy that concern and create an emotional link with voters (as opposed to making an intellectual argument)
  - The theme should explain what your candidate/campaign is while subtly showing what the opposition is not. (define both candidates/campaigns and push them farther apart)

IDENTIFY YOUR STRATEGIC OBJECTIVES:

What are the "strategic objectives" of the campaign? **In other words, "how" are you going to win?** What absolutely has to be accomplished in order to be successful? Once you determine what those objectives are, you'll want to use them as a measuring stick when deciding most everything else in the campaign.

Anything that doesn't accomplish at least one of your strategic objectives if likely to be a waste of time and resources.

☐ **List the strategic objectives that will be the PRIMARY focus of the campaign** (here are some examples)
- Targeting base vote plus switchers (1/2)
- Creating a clear difference based on perception of a single difference or essential element (2/3)
- Dividing voters along ideological lines (2/3)
- Becoming the champion of a single issue or cause (2)
- Build diverse coalitions into a voting block (1/2)
- Create a positive image (3)
- Create a negative image of opponent (3)
- Build organization capable of delivering significant vote numbers (1)
- "Buy" the election

> *Just as water alters its shape in accordance with the ground, the strategy should be flexible in order to accommodate the changing situation of the opposition. – Sun Tzu*

NOTE: *This is a general list of common objectives. There are three basic types of strategy: 1) party, 2) issue or 3) image (as noted in the list above)*

NOTE: *Customize the list to suit your campaign. You can also add vote goals for target areas/groups; priorities for finances, resources or candidate time, etc. List them in order of priority.*

STRATEGY STATEMENT:

Now you should be ready to write a general strategy statement that brings all of these elements together, keeping the "strategic formula" given below in mind.

☐ **Write a strategy statement that brings it all together.**
- **The Strategic Formula:** Candidate/campaign strengths + Opponent/campaign weaknesses divided by electorate and political environment = the ideal strategy.
- It should give the fundamental reasons your campaign will win.
- It should generally outline the types of tactics you expect to use, (remembering that any tactics you use should accomplish at least one of the "strategic objectives" that you identified above).

REVIEW THE STRATEGY:

☐ **Review your strategy by asking the following questions and make any needed adjustments**
- Does it attack the opposition's potential strategy?
- Will it help disrupt their alliances or potential alliances?
- Will it help us neutralize attacks from the opposition?
- Is the strategy <u>flexible</u>?

> *To attack the opposition's strategy is of supreme importance – Sun Tzu.*

NOTES ON THE USE OF ISSUES:

- **Voters <u>do</u> respond to issues**, "Issues win campaigns" and can either "divide" voters in your favor or "unite" them behind the opposition.
- **In order to be influenced by issues, voters must:**
  - **Be aware** of the differences between the candidates, (need sharply defined, distinctive positions). The clearer the difference, the more it influences – use issues that promote sharp division.
  - **Be motivated** to vote on the basis of that issue/or issues.

TACTICS & IMPLEMENTATION

Now that you have a strategy, you need to identify the campaign tactics that you will use, (which should revolve around the strategic goals that you identified).

ORGANIZATIONAL STRUCTURE:

Even a campaign with a great strategy won't be much of a campaign for long without good organization. Once you have decided "what" you want to do, you need a good organizational structure to define "who" will be responsible for doing it, "when", "where" and "how", etc. Below is a list of suggested items/areas you would want to find someone to put in charge of.

☐ **Create an organizational structure that reflects the campaign's strengths and likely resources with clearly defined lines of authority**
- Candidate
- Campaign Committee
- Targeting, (list development, projections, goals, profiles)
- Endorsements / key influentials
- List Development / Database manager:
    - Leadership and volunteer lists
    - Donor lists
    - Voter lists (special voter groups, etc.)
- Field Organization
- Events
- Scheduling
- Budget / Finance
- Communications
    - Media management
    - Email / newsletter copy and blasts
    - Website (and web organization efforts)
    - Social media (communications and organization)
- Speaker's Bureau (especially important for ballot campaigns)
- **Grassroots programs:** *(listed in a general campaign timeline order)*
    - Party meetings
    - District tours
    - Phone Banks (volunteer and/or voter ID)
    - Voter registration
    - Absentee ballot promotion (depending on laws in your state)
    - Yard signs
    - Door-to-door / Neighborhood blitzes
    - "Get out the vote" phone banks
    - Election Day
- Coalitions (ex. business, pro-life, Tea Party groups, etc.)
- Convention activities / organization (if applicable)

> *"The secret of all victory lies in the organization of the non-obvious."*
> *- Marcus Aurelius*

CREATING A MESSAGE:

At the end of the day, a campaign is about selling a message, and you can't really sell something that you haven't defined for yourself. It should be simple, defined in such a way as to maximize your strengths, the opposition's weaknesses, and fits with the values of the electorate. Use the items below as a guide in determining your central message points.

- ☐ **Formulate the message** (what are your central message points?)
  - Emphasize campaign strengths
  - Find the candidate's dominant characteristic or character trait and emphasize it
  - Make sure it compliments the "theme"
  - Make it relevant and compelling
  - Keep it simple and clear
  - If possible, make it actionable
  - Make sure it fits the voter's value system
  - Try to make it a dialogue *__not__* a monologue
  - Make sure it's repeated
  - Make sure our local leadership is "buying" what we're selling

- ☐ **Use the message points to create a "mission statement" and/or issues platform**
  - Eventually this is the type of information and message points you can build a "stump speech" from, as well as use as starter copy for future communications, (such as direct mail, email, website content, etc).

TYPES OF COMMUNICATIONS:

There are three basic types of media: earned, paid and owned. "Earned" means you work for it; it costs time and resources. "Paid" means just that'; you pay for it. And "owned" means you own it and can use it as and as often as you wish, (but it probably did cost you something to build at some point).

Earned media:
- Social media (likes, followers & viral sharing)
  - "Status" donations by supporters
- Press Release
- News coverage (including niche markets, blogs, etc)
- Op-Eds / Letters-to-the-editor
- Interviews
- Events
- Press conferences / announcements
- Speeches
- Debates
- Blogger relationships
- Position papers

> *"I wish people who have trouble communicating would just shut up"*
> *- Tom Lehrer*
> *(Don't be one of those people!)*

Paid media:
- Direct mail
- Email (using a professional email service, like Constant Contact or Mad Mimi)
- Internet advertising (including social media promotion)
  - Ex. Facebook ads targeted at "fans" and "friends of fans", etc.)

- PPC search marketing
- Radio ads
- TV ads
- Newspaper ads
- Billboards
- Road signs / yard signs
- Bumper stickers
- Brochures / Flyers

> *"Advertising is the very essence of democracy"*
> *- Anton Chekhov*

Owned media:
- Website / blog
- Newsletter (leveraging content from your blog)
- Social media profiles (Facebook, Twitter, etc.)
- Digital content (e-books, other downloadable resources)

ADVERTISING PRELIMINARIES:

Before spending money on paid media, take a little time to do your homework so you get the biggest bang for your buck.

- ☐ ID your market (no sense advertising to people who can't or won't vote)
- ☐ ID the costs
- ☐ Determine what your budget will allow
- ☐ Determine time availability
- ☐ Use media that compliments your message (i.e., programs that resonate with your audience)

Tips on Communications:

- *Advertising is about persuasion – and successful persuasion starts with your strategy.*
- *Given that about half of all voters split their ticket and a third make their final decision within about three weeks an election, it is important that contact is* <u>*REPETITIVE*</u> *and* <u>*PERSUASIVE*</u>.
- *Since low-level races receive less coverage there is a greater opportunity to control the type of information received by voters via paid media.*

PHONE BANKING:

When it comes to running a successful, organized phone bank, there are some basic pieces of information that you need. Like how many people are you trying to get in touch with, how much time do you have to do it in, and how long it will actually take. To figure this out, here are the basic formulas you use. Begin with the number of people that you need to contact. If this list is not "householded" (reduced to one contact per home), you start with item number 1 below. If it is, start with number 2 and work from there.

☐ **Use the formulas below to plan phone banks**

The Phone Hours Formula:
1. X voters to contact / 1.7 per household = Y
2. Y x 50% unreachable = Z reachable
3. Z / avg. 18 calls per hour = XX needed phone hours to contact them

The Phone Line Formula:
1. A call days available x B call hours per day = C available phone hours)
2. XX needed phone hours / C available hours = ___ phone lines needed.

OUTREACH & COALITIONS:

At their heart, campaigns are about people, and how best to identify, organize and communicate with them and convince them to help you accomplish a common purpose. To win. That means you need to take some time and make a special effort to reach specific groups the campaign could easily identify with and be sure the campaign message seeks to tie them together into a voting bloc.

☐ **What potential groups could we bring together in support of the campaign?**
- Occupation / trade groups
- GOP women's groups
- Tea Party groups
- Civic groups
- Can you think of others?

☐ Identify leadership & key contacts and meeting dates, (if any).

☐ Are there easy ways to reach them? (email or direct mail lists, social media, speaking, etc.?)

☐ Seek endorsements

☐ Arrange speaking opportunities

FINANCE & BUDGET:

A campaign budget is a financial picture of a campaign's priorities and how well planned and organized it is. It should be a financial map of the plans and strategy you've made so far and it should be broken out into two main categories: 1) voter contact items – expenses that involve direct contact with voters and 2) non-voter contact expenses. In a well run campaign, the vast majority of expenses fall into the "voter contact" category, (3/4's is a good standard).

☐ **Create a Budget** (some suggested items):
- **Voter Contact:**
  o Communications
  o Advertising (TV, radio, web display ads, social media, newspaper, billboards, etc.)
  o Internet / email
  o Direct mail
  o Paid phone banks
  o Grassroots programs
  o Events
  o Earned media

- **Non-Voter Contact:**
  - Salaries and consulting
  - Office / HQ rent, equipment
  - Utilities
  - Travel
  - Fundraising

"Money is the mother's milk of politics" isn't just a cliché, it's true. Now that you have a proposed budget, you've got to raise the money to fund it – which means you need a finance plan, (unless of course you're part of a "self-funded" campaign…if so, lucky you!).

☐ **Create a Finance Plan (suggested items):**
- Personal solicitation (*the candidate* is always the best fundraiser)
  - How much regular time to allocate?
  - Needs a good call list (check formers lists for leaders)
  - Someone to update data of commitments on the backend
- Finance committee (an actual *working* group!)
  - 10 to 12 people
  - High profile "chairman"
  - Director or assistant to nag for fulfillment
  - Establish agreed upon goals (for whole committee and per committee member)
  - Have regular scheduled meetings
- Special events / house parties
- Donor programs, (major & small donors)
- PAC solicitation
- Direct mail
- Website / email

> *"I have tried raising money by asking for it, and by not asking for it. I always got more by asking for it."* - Millard Fuller

TIMELINE:

A key part of any plan is having a timeline for actually putting it in motion. What happens when? Having it all on a calendar helps give everyone a view of how it all fits into the big picture – and how little time is left to get it all done. Remember, time is as much of a resource in any campaign as money or volunteers. It's finite, and each side has the same amount. A good timeline will help you make the most of it.

☐ **Create a timeline for organizational and communications programs** *(suggested items)*:
- Campaign planning process milestones
- Organization milestones
- Fundraising events and appeals (direct mail, email, candidate phone calls)
- Communications items (direct mail drops, e-blasts)
- Advertising campaigns (TV, radio, Internet, etc.)
- Grassroots programs (phone banks, neighborhood walks, yard sign blitzes, voter registration, absentee ballots, etc.)
- Get-out-the-vote programs
- Other key identified campaign goals / objectives
- Special meetings, (party, GOP Women, YR's, Tea Parties, etc.)
- Precinct meetings and county conventions, (if applicable)

NOTE: *Consider using an online calendar that you can all view securely and share with others.*
NOTE: *Work back from Election Day – space out communications*
NOTE: *Build in time for planning (ex. 1 week per planning segment)*

SAMPLE TIMELINE

TIMELINE	ITEMS

8 months out

* Campaign evaluations, research & targeting, planning & strategy complete
* Theme and message defined
* Key staff identified

7 months out

* Announcement and kick-off planned and date selected

6 months out

* Campaign finance plan completed:
  > Budget / cashflow
  > Scheduling (candidate time, events, finance committee)
  > Direct Mail
  > E-mail
* Campaign database in place (voter registraion list, etc. available)
* Coalition list in place / contacts made
* Absentee ballot program written and budgeted
* ID and turnout system defined
* Party structures incorporated

4 months out

* Grassroots organization in place
* Volunteer recruitment
* "Coalition" groups in place
* Advertising: TV, radio, Internet, etc.)
* Grassroots programs: Phone banks
* Voter registration programs

Last two months

* Grassroots programs
  > Neighborhood walks
  > Yard sign blitzes
* Absentee ballot / early voting programs
* Communications: (bi-weekly to weekly direct mail, emails twice per week)

Election Day * Get-out-the-vote activities

CAMPAIGN UPDATES:

Of course planning a campaign is just the beginning. **Once things are under way, don't make the mistake of just going from day to day and not taking time to stop and review how things are going.** I've added a simple review form in the appendix that you should be able to use for regular campaign updates, (weekly or monthly, depending on the campaign and how close you are to Election Day).

Make blank copies of the campaign review form so that you can use it at regular campaign planning meetings.

Good luck with your campaign!

Campaign Review & Update   DATE: _____

ORGANIZATION:

_____ - Are all precincts / counties covered with a campaign chairman?
_____ - Are volunteer recruitment efforts being effective?
_____ - Are church contacts being identified?
_____ - Are we focusing on our "target" areas?
_____ - Does the database meet our current and anticipated needs?
_____ - Is there a good delegation of duties / structure?
_____ - Is there "Harmony of the Host" with the leadership? Are they all on the same page?
_____ - Do we have the resources we need? Are we using them well?
_____ - Are we using the candidate's time well?
_____ - Are we able to recognize changing circumstances and act expediently?

COMMUNICATIONS:

_____ - Does our message work?
_____ - Are our communications and advertising efforts on schedule?
_____ - Is our communications schedule "timely"?
_____ - Do our efforts effectively communicate our message?
Current / Planned Communications: _____
_____

What are the current results of the "Voter ID" phone banks?
_____ - ID'd "Favorable"
_____ - ID'd "Against"
_____ - ID'd "Undecided"
_____ - Total number of contacts
_____ - Do we have good availability of phone lines and volunteers?

STRATEGY:

_____ - Is our strategy still relevant to the current situation? Does our plan still work?
_____ - Do all of our efforts and activities accomplish some aspect of our strategy?
_____ - Do our current plans make good use of the calendar?

BUDGET / FUNDRAISING:

_____ - What is the current cash-on-hand?
_____ - Anticipated expenses? _____ - Expected revenues? _____ - Difference +/-
_____ - Do we have enough to fund our plan?
_____ - Are any other fund-raisers on the schedule?
_____ - Has a Finance Committee been formed? Does it meet? Does it have goals?
_____ - Are we using our money well?

INDICATORS:

_____- If there has been any polling, are the results favorable?
_____- Are we making good progress with targeted groups?
_____- Do we have unity among our natural base of support? What are they saying?
_____
_____

ISSUES:

What are the most important issues? Any recent changes? _____
_____

OPPOSITION:

What is the opposition's strategy? Is it effective? Any changes? _____
_____

Has there been any communications or advertising from the opposition? _____
_____

Has the opposition attacked our candidate? _____
_____

____- Have we responded?
_____- Have our responses been effective?

How organized is the opposition?_____
_____

How well financed is the opposition? _____
_____

POLITICAL CLIMATE:

Other political forces or circumstances that could impact the campaign? _____
_____

How can we accommodate and/or use of them to our advantage? _____
_____

Is the road ahead easy of difficult? _____
_____

MISC:

_____
_____
_____

Did you find this book useful?
If so, help spread the word and let other conservatives know about it. Send them a link to http://DrewMcKissick.com and tell them about it!

Want more?
If you're ready to learn more, you can check out my Grassroots 101 Training Series, (available on my website). It's your three volume guide to the fundamentals of grassroots politics!

Stay Connected!
Be sure that you sign up for my free newsletter at http://DrewMcKissick.com with more grassroots tips and occasional conservative commentary. You can also find me at: http://facebook.com/DrewMcKissickPage and @DrewMcKissick on Twitter.

About Drew McKissick
"Helping conservatives make a difference!"

I'm a conservative activist with over twenty-five years of experience in grassroots politics and a passion for teaching others how the system works and how to become effective.

Professionally, my work involves specializing in political strategy, planning and organization as well as the development of grassroots related political action programs. I also write a regular column offering grassroots tips and political commentary.

I got involved in politics years ago because I cared about issues, and I decided that I could have the greatest impact on those issues by getting involved in the Republican Party and working to keep it focused on conservative principles and helping good conservative candidates get elected to office.

I am a former member of the Republican National Committee (from SC), a long time conservative political activist at the local, state and national levels and have been an active member of the SC Republican Party for over twenty-five years. I've been able to serve in elected and appointed positions at all levels of our party, and have been involved in all aspects of the GOP's organization.

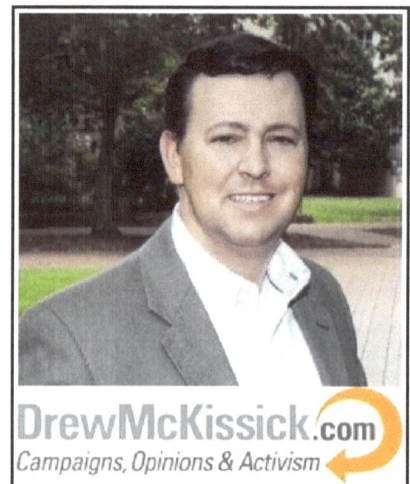

You can find me online at:
DrewMcKissick.com
Facebook.com/DrewMcKissickPage
Twitter.com/DrewMcKissick